RIVERS
ALL LEADERS
MUST CROSS

Entering into a
Promising Tomorrow

LIFE IMPACT SERIES

FRANK DAMAZIO

CITYCHRISTIAN
PUBLISHING
www.CityChristianPublishing.com

PUBLISHED BY CITY CHRISTIAN PUBLISHING
9200 NE Fremont, Portland, Oregon 97220

City Christian Publishing is a ministry of City Bible Church and is dedicated to serving
the local church and its leaders through the production and distribution of quality
equipping resources. It is our prayer that these materials, proven in the context of the
local church, will equip leaders in exalting the Lord and extending His kingdom.

For a free catalog of additional resources from City Christian Publishing, please call
1-800-777-6057 or visit our web site at www.CityChristianPublishing.com.

Rivers All Leaders Must Cross
© Copyright 2006 by Frank Damazio
All Rights Reserved
ISBN: 1-59383-033-5

First Edition, January 2006

Printed in the United States of America

CONTENTS

Leaders entering new territory must carry with them stones to build a solid foundation for their Kingdom endeavors. These include foundational stones of humility, prayer, healing, miracles, and spiritual warfare. With these and other stones of truth, leaders will be prepared for the responsibility and challenge of God's calling and purpose.

Part 1

Preparing for the Journey

Then Joshua rose early in the morning; and they set out from Acacia Grove and came to the Jordan, he and all the children of Israel, and lodged there before they crossed over.—Joshua 3:1

Joshua came to the edge of the Jordan, a river of destiny for the people of God. The crossing drew a line in their history—the dawn of a new day, the unfolding of a new purpose. Throughout time, God's people have been called to cross rivers and take cities. Israel's Canaan had walled cities, numerous gods, temples, and cultic practices. All were to be rooted out.

We also stand on the edge of a river ready to cross over into our Canaan—into regions with fortresses raised against God, with immoral standards and cultic worship of human-made idols.

Carl F. Henry, the noted historian and theologian, paints our cultural picture with clarity when he writes:

> The unraveling strands of western civilization are everywhere. . . . The inability to cope publicly with drug use and traffic is painfully apparent. On every hand, one sees moral deterioration and ethical upheaval, together with attendant manifestations of melancholy and hopelessness. Amid the deteriorating cultural configurations, moral permissiveness has spawned lives scarred

and marred by illegitimate sex and adultery, homosexuality and pornography.[1]

The Edge, the Overflow and the Harvest

The crossing of Jordan is set out in Joshua 3 and 4. There were doubtless special reasons that induced Joshua to cross Jordan at the lower fords opposite Jericho rather than higher up the river—an easier crossing that led directly into central Palestine. His decision was probably influenced by a desire to possess a fortified base at Jericho and in the neighboring cities.

The timing of Joshua's crossing is of prophetic importance. Scripture expressly states that the Israelites approached the river at the time of harvest in the early spring. The time of harvest was also a time when the water level would rise to flood stage and would fill the entire channel from bank to bank. Signs all around us are bearing witness that the water level is rising. The water level for God's people is an ever-growing revival spirit filling our churches, cities, and nations.

Worldwide, church growth has been impressive. Less than five percent of the population of Africa professed Christianity at the turn of the twentieth century. By the year 2000, 50 percent of Africa's population was Christian. China had only about five million believers when communist rule took control of the country. Now the estimates vary from 50 to as high as 150 million believers. Estimates are that 25,000 and 35,000 are coming to Christ daily in China.[2]

We are standing on the edge of our rivers to cross into the future. Church history records providential seasons when God seems manifestly to go before His people, expecting His people to follow. There must be no hesitation, no room for excuses, no resistance to moving forward.

Only God Can Take Us Across the River

The ordinary methods of prayer, worship, and ministry will not be sufficient for this season of moving through and over these new revival rivers. Like Joshua and God's people in the Old Testament, we must cross over *by following the manifest presence of God.* In Joshua's day, the Ark of God set out first and then the leaders followed the Ark into the waters of the Jordan, as recorded in Joshua 3:14, 15:

> So it was, when the people set out from their camp to cross over the Jordan, with the priests bearing the ark of the covenant before the people, and as those who bore the ark came to the Jordan, and the feet of the priests who bore the ark dipped in the edge of the water (for the Jordan overflows all its banks during the whole time of harvest).

His presence may lead us in most unusual ways, especially during revival seasons, to get us into the flood waters of the Jordan (the river of God). Stepping into a river flowing at flood stage is not the normal way to cross a river. It poses many dangers and raises many fears. We may fear that we will be swept away in the rising waters. We may fear that we will lose the security of standing on the banks, but we must trust God's manifest presence. We set out. We let go. We wade into the water.

The Symbolic Reference of Rivers

Scripture commonly uses rivers as symbols of God's presence or His Spirit (Ps. 1:1-3; John 7:37-39; Rev. 22:1), but rivers can also be used to symbolize other biblical themes. One Hebrew word for river is *nahal*, meaning a torrent valley. Summer's dry riverbed or ravine would become a raging torrent during the rainy season. The River Jabbok

(Deut. 2:37) was such a river, as were all the streams mentioned in Elijah's stories. Because these river-beds could suddenly become raging torrents, they often came to symbolize the pride of nations (see Isa. 66:12), the strength of the invader (Jer. 47:2), and the power of the enemy (see Ps. 124:4).[3]

The river of God is seen in the Garden of Eden (see Gen. 2:10), in Ezekiel's Temple (Ezek. 47:1-10), in the believer (John 7:37-39), and in the new city of God (Rev. 22:1). All of these representations easily demonstrate the power of God's presence to bring new life and fruitfulness.

The New Testament uses rivers to symbolize the salvation of God, the life or power of God, and the Holy Spirit's impartation and cleansing (John 3:5; 4:13, 14; 7:37-39; 13:10; Titus 3:5). In the new city of God (Rev. 22:1-5), the pure water comes from the throne of God for the healing of the na-tions.[4]

The river of God that flows to God's people is an outpouring of His Spirit for the purpose of bringing healing to the nations, to our sick and dying culture. We desperately need a deep and living river of God in our struggling churches worldwide. We need a refreshing river for a discouraged and disconnected twenty-first-century Church. We need God's river!

Jordan, the River of Death and Life

The Jordan River depression is a unique geographical formation. Formed as a result of a rift valley, it is the lowest depression on earth. Thus the name Jordan in the Hebrew, *Yarden*, aptly means "the descender." The Jordan River is the largest watercourse in Palestine; its distance of some 75 miles to the Dead Sea is more than doubled by its meandering path.

No other river has more biblical allusions and

significance. In Christian hymns and preaching, the Jordan River has often symbolized the transition of death from this life to the next. The Jordan River also represented a death of sorts to the Hebrew children. Prophetically, it represents a river we all must pass through each time we embrace revival rivers.

Revival rivers bring a death to self, to pride, and to our natural strength. Before Joshua could take the cities of Canaan, he and the people had to pass through the Jordan, which was a river of death before it could become a river of life.

We, like Namaan of old, must be willing to dip seven times in rivers to shed our old self and its carnalities. Only when we are willing to accept ALL that He has for us can we be made whole.

Namaan's Response to the Jordan

And Elisha sent a messenger to him, saying,

"Go and wash in the Jordan seven times, and your flesh shall be restored to you, and you shall be clean" (2 Kings 5:10).

A simple message given to Namaan caused a furious response:

But Namaan became furious, and went away and said, "Indeed, I said to myself, 'He will surely come out to me, and stand and call on the name of the LORD his God, and wave his hand over the place, and heal the leprosy'" (2 Kings 5:11).

His thinking was: *Couldn't I dip myself in the Abanah or Pharpar Rivers, the rivers of Damascus? Aren't they better than all the rivers in Israel?* We too may be challenged to dip into rivers that are not of our making and not of our choosing. Yet they are rivers that God has chosen to bring restoration and life to us.

What was it that finally convinced Namaan to

dip in the muddy Jordan, the river he disliked by reputation and by natural understanding? It was a desperation and a willingness to be humbled. Yes, a little swallowing of his military self-will and pompous attitude. A lesser leader encouraged him by saying, in effect, "If the prophet had told you to do something hard, impossible, unbearable, wouldn't you have done it? So why not do it when all he says to you is 'Wash, and be clean'?" This reasoning caused the great Namaan to humble himself enough to go down and dip seven times in the muddy, dirty, undesirable Jordan. Not once. Not twice. Seven times. He was asked to dip in the Jordan until he was thoroughly saturated by the Jordan River.

Every river of revival has its good and bad, its human and divine. This mixture causes some to respond, like Namaan, with a "No, not that river. How could God bless that river with all its obvious flaws, human carnality, and shallow doctrine?

It doesn't make sense." Contrary to our understanding, the ways of the Spirit are not always logical or rational. Nevertheless, we must drink deeply from all rivers sent by the Holy Spirit.

In the words of Joshua 3:1: "And came to the Jordan. . . . and lodged there before they crossed over." We must lodge at the river.

Lodging at the River

Revival necessitates two steps: (1) lodging at the river and (2) crossing over. Some might take the first step and never move to the second, so enthralled and satisfied with the lodging that they have no desire for the crossing. Others will desire only the crossing of the river, never allowing any time to lodge at the river. We must do both. This is not just revival wisdom—it is spiritually healthy—a matter of life or death.

The word lodge used in Joshua 3:1 means to

stop and stay for a length of time, to lie down and stay still, to patiently remain and tarry. When the Holy Spirit is doing something new and fresh, the greatest need is to lodge. The greatest gift during revival times is not necessarily the gift of leadership, but the gift of fellowship. Knowing that we do not have all the answers creates a holy desperation which is found by those who lodge at the river and are willing to keep dipping into the new, sometimes uncomfortable, thing that God is asking them to experience.

Whether we're in full-time church ministry as a pastor, elder, or missionary or a secular ministry such as a carpenter, electrician, or sales person, we all need to lodge at the river. We need to camp out with God. We need to take time, be patient, wait on God by praying, fasting, worshipping, being cleansed through repentance, and by hearing God's Word with an open heart. As the spiritual flow of the Holy Spirit increases in our midst, we will have the opportunity to drink from that river, receiving newness of spirit, soul, and body. We must develop a personal love and commitment to drink deeply of revival rivers as God allows them to flow near us and through us.

Lodging: God's Cure for Spiritual Drought

Spiritually dry souls in desert places are prime candidates for the refreshing river of God. A person, family, church, or group of churches may be in a spiritual drought, in desperate need of a genuine spiritual awakening, in need of the river of God. Perhaps you can identify:

My vitality was turned into the drought of summer (Ps. 32:4).

My soul thirsts for You; my flesh longs for You in a dry and thirsty land where there is no water (Ps. 63:1).

The word "drought" means a continuous dry wind that blows rain clouds away, scorching the ground; a restraint of refreshing rain for long periods of time; an extended dryness in the heat of summer. "Dry," "thirsty," "rainless," and "hardened" are words that may describe your soul or the spiritual state of your church. In the natural, when a region has had a long drought, the ground becomes so hardened that the first rains will not penetrate it. Instead the first downpour can result in flash floods as the hardened ground resists the water. Several rains are needed to soften the ground. The first gentle rains begin to soften the ground slowly. Then, as additional rains come, penetrating rains, the ground softens more and more, accepting more of the water instead of repelling it. Finally, rains begin to fall that will be absorbed, soaking deeply into the ground, readying it for the seed to be planted and to produce fruit.

So it is with dry souls and dry churches. We

need softening rains, penetrating rains and rains that will be absorbed. The Word of God promises refreshing water to those who are in a dry and thirsty place:

> He opened the rock, and water gushed out;
> it ran in the dry places like a river (Ps. 105:41).

> He turns a wilderness into pools of water,
> and dry land into watersprings (Ps. 107:35).

> For I will pour water on him who is thirsty, and floods on the dry ground; I will pour My Spirit on your descendants, and My blessing on your offspring (Isa. 44:3; see also Isa. 32:1,2; 41:17,18; Matt. 12:43).

Our responsibility is to stop, lodge, or drink deeply of the rivers of God (Jer. 31:12). Lodging may sound like a trivial point to enlarge upon, but I see it as one of the foundational steps to entering into revival rivers in the twenty-first century. We must not only come to the edge (Josh. 3:15), but we must also wade out into the waters God has made available to us and drink deeply and personally of that water. To drink means to absorb, consume, take in. Drinking speaks of openness (Deut. 11:11; Jer. 31:12; John 4:14, 7:37-39; Eph. 5:18).

Prepare your heart, mind, and spirit with expectation and faith to receive (2 Kings 3:16, 17). Dig out a place for the Holy Spirit to fill up. Open your hands. Open your spirit. Drink. Absorb. Let the breath of God's Spirit breathe new life into you (John 20:22) and receive power from on high for the crossing (Acts 1:8).

Personal Application

1. As we are seeing concurrent levels of revival and evil waters rising, we must be willing to tear down the false idols that attempt to crowd

out the Lord of the Harvest. What idols do you need to reckon with in order to maintain a soul-winning focus?

2. Most of us have blind areas where we are sure that our doctrines and denominations are the river rather than tributaries that contribute to the river. Will you ask the Holy Spirit to expose any veiled areas of pride or rigidity in you?

3. Can you relate to Naaman? What outrageous ideas has God asked you to accept that you refuse to dip into as part of God's solution for taking you to the Promised Land?

4. Before any of us can bring the refreshing waters of revival to others, we must be refreshed ourselves. Are you lodging in God's presence? If not, could it be that you need to bring your self-effort into the Jordan?

NOTES

1. Carl F. Henry, *Gods of This Age or God of the Ages* (Nashville: Broadman Holman Publishers, 1992), p. 2.

2. Neil Anderson and Elmer Towns, *Rivers of Revival* (Ventura, CA: Renew Books, 1997), pp. 12, 15.

3. J. D. Douglas, *The New Bible Dictionary* (Grand Rapids: Wm. B. Eerdman's Publishing Company, 1974), p. 1098.

4. Frank E. Gaebelein, *Expositor's Bible Commentary, New International Version, Volume 2* (Grand Rapids: Zondervan, 1992), p. 599.

Part 2

SUMMONING STRENGTH
FOR THE CROSSING

They set out from Acacia Grove and came to the Jordan, he and all the children of Israel, and lodged there before they crossed over.—Joshua 3:1

As we embrace our Jordan and prepare for this journey, we move into our future and grasp our destiny. The cities before us are tightly shut up to heaven, sealed by evil influences and invisible powers. These places are our inheritance, our challenge, our future, but we need a fresh anointing of God's Holy Spirit, a fresh, supernatural, city-reaching power to secure that inheritance.

Revivals come to first transform the Church and then transform the unsaved world. God must come and be received by His own people before He can be proclaimed to the unsaved. Revival rivers were never meant to be captured and owned by the Church alone. Rivers of revival are to flow out from the house of God into every valley, wilderness, desert, and walled city. We, as Joshua did, must come to the edge of each revival river and prepare ourselves to step into the river and to cross over the river, taking with us new power, new truths, new faith, and new vision.

The Acacia Grove, a Boot Camp for the Crossing

The preparation for embracing new movements of God's Holy Spirit and then assimilating those outpourings into our lives, ministries, and churches starts with cleansing. Joshua 3:1 says, "and they set out from Acacia Grove and came to the Jordan." The Acacia Grove experience is foundational to moving to the edge of the river and stepping in to cross over it.

Acacia wood was named for its durability. In the Hebrew, the word "acacia" means non-decaying, durable, and was sometimes translated "incorruptible wood" in the Septuagint. The Acacia Grove experience is a fresh and life-changing encounter with true biblical holiness. Holiness and the twenty-first-century, modern-day culture are destined to clash in every way possible. The shifts that have occurred in today's value system have been mega shifts. The humanistic, syncretistic philosophy of our world culture has eroded all moral value systems. We now face a new culture, a new Canaan, a culture separated from God and His Word.

If the Acacia Grove experience is ignored, avoided, or found to be distasteful to those seeking revival, then revival will be a mixture of flesh and spirit and is destined to be shallow and short lived. The very core of our Christian living must be examined, cleansed, and changed if we are to cross the rivers of God and touch entire cities for Christ. A stop at Acacia is not optional!

Holiness, the Fruit of the Acacia Grove

Holiness is one of the most frequent descriptive terms used of God. The Lord is called "the Holy One" more than 30 times in Isaiah alone. The word "holy" occurs more than 600 times in the Bible, and one entire book, Leviticus, is devoted to the subject of holiness. As we can see from the following Scriptures, God places a high premium on holiness and demands personal and corporate holiness from His people.

Pursue peace with all men, and *holiness*, without which no one will see the Lord (Heb. 12:14, italics added).

Therefore, having these promises, beloved, let us *cleanse ourselves* from all filthiness of the flesh and spirit, perfecting *holiness* in the fear of God (2 Cor. 7:1, italics added).

But as He who called you is *holy*, you also be *holy* in all your conduct, because it is written, "Be holy, for I am holy" (1 Pet. 1:15, 16, italics added).

I speak in human terms because of the weakness of your flesh. For just as you presented your members as slaves of uncleanness, and of lawlessness leading to more lawlessness, so now present your members as slaves of righteousness for holiness (Rom. 6:19).

The word "holiness" causes many different responses and reactions in today's Church. People may conjure up bad memories of hellfire and brimstone messages, hammering on hairstyles, modern make-up, dress styles, and entertainment taboos. True holiness, however, is God's idea and therefore must be attainable and spiritually satisfying to all believers who seek God.

The primary meaning of holy is "separate." It comes from an ancient word that means to cut or separate. In contemporary language, we would use the phrase "to cut apart" or "a cut above." *Strong's Concordance* defines holy as "morally blameless."[1] *Vine's Expository Dictionary* states, "Holiness is separated to God from sin with conduct befitting one so separated."[2] A. W. Pink says, "Holiness consists of that internal change or renovation of our souls whereby our minds, affections, and wills are brought into harmony with God."[3]

The Hebrew verb *qadash* is translated in various ways throughout the Old Testament: to dedicate, hallow, consecrate, sanctify, set apart, keep holy, make holy, and to purify.

In order to move toward a river of God's power and presence, whether it be a national revival river or the river of God that we encounter every Sunday when we come together, we must visit the Acacia Grove for cleansing, purifying and releasing. Second Corinthians 7:1 confirms this: "Therefore, having these promises, beloved, let us cleanse ourselves from all filthiness of the flesh and spirit, perfecting holiness in the fear of God." (See also Lev. 11:44; 1 Sam. 16:5; John 17:16, 17; 2 Tim. 2:2; Heb. 2:11.)

The Collision of Holiness and Culture

Holiness is in direct confrontation with a culture gone astray. We are ruled by the notion that life somehow gives us the right to have every whim and desire fulfilled. We live in a world that believes in exhausting itself on the mistaken notion that physical pleasures produce happiness. Our nation dismisses the idea of the wrath of God as a product of puritan prudishness. The widespread belief is that moral absolutes are nothing more than psychological hang-ups. We desperately need a long stop at the Acacia Grove to return to the biblical concepts of holiness, purity, and godly standards.

Chuck Colson agrees:

It strikes me that the prevalent characteristic of our culture today is rampant narcissism, materialism, and hedonism. Our culture passes itself off as Christian with 50 million Americans, according to George Gallup, claiming to be born again. But it is dominated almost entirely by relativism.

The do-your-own-thing mind-set has liberated us from the absolute structure of faith and belief and set us adrift in a sea of nothingness.[4]

We are challenged, but not discouraged, to be living in such a culture, for all around us are signs of God desiring to bring a revival of truth, right thinking, godly values, and a Church victorious and conquering. As we pursue holiness, let us with knowledge lay aside those philosophies that may hinder our pursuit.

Therefore we also, since we are surrounded by so great a cloud of witnesses, let us lay aside every weight, and the sin which so easily ensnares us, and let us run with endurance the race that is set before us, looking unto Jesus, the author and finisher of our faith, who for the joy that was set before Him endured the cross, despising the shame, and has sat down at the right hand of the throne of God (Heb. 12:1, 2).

Exposing Modern-Day Hindrances

At the Acacia Grove, cop-out practices and philosophies that have subtly and insidiously infiltrated the Church culture with too much religion and too little relationship are exposed and reckoned with. The following are just a few that keep us from stepping into our Jordan of destiny.

- **Legalism:** Legalism hinders believers by squeezing every decision into a strict and often overly literalistic interpretation of the Scriptures (or church tradition). For a legalist, rules and regulations are seen as directives to be meticulously followed, rather than guidelines or principles to be applied with wisdom and insight in varying circumstances. In its worst form, legalism assumes that salvation itself can be earned by the work of following God's laws—a mockery of the New Testament teaching on the helplessness of humans to do works pleasing to God apart from the mercy and grace of God through Jesus Christ.

- **Libertarianism:** Libertarianism begins with a person freely creating his or her own standards and values, expressing them in words and action, without having to be burdened by timeless principles, maxims or rules; one must rely on self alone for the correct ethical course. This is not a new philosophy; it can be seen as the understanding by which Israel brought disaster upon itself, everyone doing "what was right in his own eyes" (Judg. 17:6; Prov. 12:15).

- **Existentialism:** Like libertarianism, existentialism rejects what it regards as abstract moral truths given by God or gods in favor of the concrete existence of humans and whatever values or ethics they have chosen. Existentialism emphasizes that, in each present moment, we as individuals are totally free and must, by the force of will, create our own meaning. Existentialism claims that, to make authentic choices, we cannot rely on our reason, which leads us only to disagreements and paradoxes. Instead, we must rely on our inner (irrational) consciousness. Jean-Paul Sartre, the most famous proponent of existentialism, said, "Man is condemned to freedom." This total freedom creates anxiety about the realization of absolute nonexistence after death and about no God and no judgment. Existentialists rely on their gut feelings rather than absolute truth. They rely on themselves rather than God. Existentialism places the priority on the emotional rather than reason, asking, "How can it be wrong if it feels so right?"

- **Situational Ethics:** The situational ethicist enters every decision-making situation with the assumption that the situation heavily influences ethical decisions and can even overturn existing moral precepts. The highest value for situational ethicists is usually described as "love." If a person embraces this philosophy, biblical holiness is impossible because true holiness begins with the absolute Word of God.

- **Pragmatism:** Pragmatism says that whatever brings satisfaction and whatever works is right and good. Pragmatism expresses one of the main inspirations of American culture and of the techno-scientific era. To a pragmatist, the end justifies the means.

- **Relativism:** Relativism has many forms; the main idea is that "what's true or right for you may or may not be what's true or right for me." Relativism can be expressed as cultural relativism, ethical relativism, and relativism of personal worlds. In relativism, there are no objective standards of truth or justice; everything is relative.

- **Humanism:** Secular humanism dethrones God as the center of life and enshrines humanity instead. The tenets of humanism are atheism, evolution, amorality, autonomous man, and a socialist, one-world view. Regarding amorality, the Humanist Manifesto says, "In the area of sexuality, we believe that intolerant attitudes are often cultivated by orthodox religions, which unduly repress sexual conduct. The right to birth control, abortion, and divorce should be recognized. Neither do we wish to prohibit sexual behavior between consenting adults."

When you put biblical holiness, which is founded upon biblical absolutes, up against a tidal wave of non-biblical philosophies, you feel the overwhelming pressure of encouraging a livable holiness.

As a pastor of a multigenerational, multiethnic church in a fairly large city, I am—as we all are—faced with every kind of sinful enticement. Our congregation is conservative about moral standards and biblical convictions regarding entertainment and lifestyle in general. We preach and teach against moral looseness, sinful behavior, and habits and take a clear stand against premarital sex, adultery, and any other clear moral sin. Our pastors, counselors, lay pastors, small group leaders, youth leaders, and college leaders all have some form of accountability and a clear standard for living as leaders. Yet, with all of this, it is absolutely amazing how much sin, sinful behavior, unbroken sinful lifestyle patterns, and unconfessed moral failure exist at some level in our congregation.

I believe that every church battles with these same laws of degeneration. Some pastors, leaders, bishops, and elders may become discouraged and overwhelmed with the struggle of leading a congregation into biblical holiness. This is exactly why we must always journey to our Acacia Grove, our place of touching the holiness of God, receiving the newness of life that conquers the old.

The Bible does call the believer a saint, a word that simply means holy one. We might stumble over this, but the Scripture says that we pastors lead holy people—some with foolish and sinful behaviors. At all times, our holiness is found in our position in Christ first. We must claim Christ's perfection as we deal with our imperfections and we must expect a continual and gradual work of sanctification.

In one of our services, I instructed the congregation to write down privately a sin or sins that were besetting them: lifestyles, habit patterns, or weaknesses. We then spent time on our knees confessing, repenting, and asking God for cleansing, deliverance, and freedom. After our time of repentance, I asked the church to bring these pieces of paper forward and deposit them in two large trash cans at the altar. We experienced a very unusual sense of God's grace and power as people placed their sins in the trash can. I then had the pieces of paper burned and collected the ashes and put them into a bottle that sits on my desk. You may think this is strange, but it is a reminder to me that our congregation has given up these ashes in order to receive the beauty of the Lord (see Isa. 61:1-4). This congregation, with all our defects and faults, is claiming God's miracle-working grace to take the best or worst of our sins and turn them into ashes, giving us His beauty.

Acacia Grove Principles

There are no set formulas for livable holiness, but there are clear biblical principles to follow. The following are just a few of the principles that come from the Acacia Grove:

- Everything is permissible for me, but everything is not beneficial (see 1 Cor. 6:12).

- Everything is permissible for me, but I will not be mastered by anything. I will not allow anything to bring me under its power (see 1 Cor. 6:12).

- If something is permissible, but hurts other people, I will refrain (see 1 Cor. 8:13).

- In everything I do, I will purpose to bring glory to God (see 1 Cor. 10:31).

- I will keep my thoughts lined up with the Word of God. My thoughts are as important as my actions (see 1 Sam. 16:7; Ps. 139:1-4; Prov. 23:7; Phil. 4:8).

- I will transform my habits into godly disciplines for living (see Rom. 6:19; 12:1, 2; 2 Tim. 3:16).

We concur that holiness is the believer's separation from the cares, lusts, and carnal culture of the world around us in response to God's call to be holy people who are set apart unto God. This holy calling is a sovereign act of God, whereas the perfecting of holiness is an ongoing, everyday, gradual, continual responsibility of every believer and every church. As we continually desire to enter into the river of God's presence and purpose, we make a commitment to holiness; we choose the Acacia Grove.

Your testimonies are very sure; holiness adorns Your house, O LORD, forever (Ps. 93:5).

I Cry Holy

By Mark Strauss

I see Your throne lifted high;
Angels bow down giving glory.
I hear a multitude cry:
"Holy, holy!"

Lord, by Your grace, I draw near;
I join this heavenly chorus,
Echoing that which I hear:
"Holy, holy, holy, Lord!"

I cry, "Holy, holy!"
You're the spotless Lamb,
The sinless Son of Man.
I cry, "Holy, holy!"

You have paid the price with Your sacrifice.
In You, I stand complete
To worship at Your feet.
I cry, "Holy, holy, Lord!"[5]

Personal Application

1. On a scale of 1 to 10, how important is holiness to you? Does your life reflect that kind of holiness?

2. Christians sometimes sacrifice loving relationship for rules that elevate the tree of the knowledge of good and evil. When that happens, we bring judgment (legalism) rather than grace to others. Can you identify any modern-day philosophies and practices that have subtly influenced your thinking, causing you to compromise God's Word?

3. Set aside a moment to list your besetting sins. (If you think you don't have any, consider listing pride.) Burn the list and ask God to bring something good out of your ashes.

4. Reread the Acacia Grove principles. Which ones do you need to realign with before stepping into your river of destiny?

Notes

1. *Strong's Exhaustive Concordance of the Bible* (New York: Abingdon Press, 1890), p. 7.

2. W. E. Vine, *Vine's Expository Dictionary of New Testament Words* (London: Oliphants, 1957), p. 2251.

3. A. W. Pink, *The Doctrine of Sanctification* (Evangel, PA: Bible Truth Depot, 1955), p. 7.

4. Chuck Colson, source unknown.

5. Mark Strauss, "I Cry Holy," City Bible Music, 1997. Used with permission.

Part 3

ENTERING THE RIVERS
OF RENEWAL

*When you have come to the edge of the water of the
Jordan, you shall stand in the Jordan.*—Joshua 3:8

The crossing of rivers for the contemporary
Church is the embracing of present-day Holy
Spirit waters that could be classified revival rivers.
Revival rivers have been present in most generations
and the Church has always had the choice of moving
into the river, bypassing the river, ignoring the river,

or reacting to the river. When a generation reacts to or misses the river of God, it may be a Judges 2:10 generation: "Another generation arose after them who did not know the LORD, nor the work which He had done for Israel." Reverend Bevon Jones states, "Never let a generation grow up without that knowledge of divine things, which may contain the germ of national revival in years to come."[1]

Portraits of Revivals Past

Every generation has the potential to experience a generation gap or a revival gap. We face it today as did previous generations—the cycle of change and decay, of reformation and apostasy. To break in upon this cycle of decline, God sends revivals, rivers of His Holy Spirit to awaken and revive His people.

Each generation has had its chosen leaders, reformers, and revivalists who were used to turn the

Church toward the river of revival. In the dark days of the twelfth century, there was Frances of Assisi who, in his brown monk's robe, used words like a sword to pierce the heart. In the fourteenth century, Savanarola, a man steeped in the Scriptures and in the Holy Spirit, called his generation to repentance. He was a fasting, praying, prophetic preacher who spoke with the fire power of the Holy Spirit, affecting his generation. The reformer Martin Luther (1483-1546) touched his generation with his powerful messages and leadership in a reformation that changed the course of history. Martin Luther embraced the river of God, crossed through the river, and reached his generation with revival-reformation truths. By 1517, Luther gave us the basic framework of present Protestant theology. He had been convinced of three basic points:

- A man is justified by faith alone and not by works.

- Each believer has access to God directly, apart from any human intermediaries.
- The Bible is the supreme source of authority for both faith and life.

God is deeply committed to visit each and every generation with His divine presence and power. We could go on and on, speaking of John and Charles Wesley, George Whitfield, Ludwig von Zinzendorf, John Calvin, Charles Finney, Jonathan Edwards, D. L. Moody, and the Great Awakenings in our own nation. Revival rivers have always been available— disguised, unlikely, outside our camp, but always there. The 1905-1906 Awakening rolled like a tidal wave through our nation and around the world. Pentecostal denominations find their beginnings in this turn-of-the-century revival. Again we are faced with many different rivers of revival. Some may be only rills, brooks, or small streams. Others may be raging rivers of Holy Spirit power and presence.

Portraits of Revivals

The people and places that have taken on national and international interest have been a source of controversy to many, of blessing to thousands, and possibly of rivers of revival for the Church. These are people such as Rodney Howard-Browne of South Africa who arrived in the United States in 1987 and made an impact in many parts of our nation as well as in the Philippines, Singapore, Russia, and Africa. People have rejected and attacked Rodney for the "Laughing Revival" just as passionately as others have received him.

John and Carol Arnott of Toronto, Canada, invited Randy Clark to hold revival meetings that began January 20, 1994—meetings which continued for many years afterwards. The Toronto Blessing touched thousands with a new love for God, for the Holy Spirit, and for the simplicity of receiving more of Jesus. Leaders from many nations arrived in Toronto to drink from the waters of this revival; they came from Switzerland, Germany, France, Sweden, Norway, England, Scotland, and more, as well as most major cities in the United States and Canada. All were affected by this unusual outburst of God's river.

Many thousands have been blessed, churches have been transformed, and pastors by the thousands have testified to a revived heart for God and His Holy Spirit. Yet some were offended and confused, blatantly rejecting the movements and calling this river a counterfeit revival. Hank Hanegraaf, in his book *Counterfeit Revival*, makes strong accusations that some revivals are more similar to cults than to works of God:

What can Heaven's Gate, Waco, and Jonestown have in common with a church near you?

As incredible as it may seem, the principles

used by leaders of cults are today employed in literally thousands of churches worldwide. Tactics once relegated to the ashrams of cults are now replicated at the altars of churches—as Christians worldwide ape the practices of pagan spirituality. . . . Socio-psychological manipulation tactics such as Altered states of consciousness, Peer pressure, Exploitation of expectations, and Subtle suggestions (A-P-E-S) are so powerful they can cause human beings to "behave like beasts or idiots and be proud of it." No one is immune—once an epidemic of hysteria is in full force, it can make black appear white, obscure realities, enshrine absurdities, and cause people to die with purple shrouds over their corpses.[2]

Hank Hanegraaf's evaluation may be an extreme reaction to rivers of revival, but it is part of mainstream Christianity's thinking. Some of his concerns are valid, but some of his conclusions could be a mixture of fear and carnal reaction. Whether you feel as strongly as Hank Hanegraaf or only have doubts and questions as to the validity of these revivals, you are still faced with their existence.

For instance, another river of revival took place at Brownsville Assembly of God in Brownsville, Florida on Father's Day, June 18, 1995. Evangelist Steve Hill was invited to speak that Sunday at Brownsville Assembly. Revival broke out and stayed. Thousands have answered the salvation altar call and multiplied thousands have rededicated their lives to Christ. Almost 2 million people have passed through the doors of Brownsville Assembly.[3]

The book *Revival* by John Arnott, Malcolm McDow, and Alvin Reid records the stories of revival rivers on college campuses. Revival has spread to college and university campuses with countless reports of repentance, reconciliation, restored relationships, thousands of salvations, and prodigals returning to the Lord from Indiana Wesleyan College in Marion, Indiana, Biola University in Los Angeles, California, and dozens of others.[4]

The reports of revival are varied and numerous; another revival to embrace, another river to cross.

Testing the Waters of Revival

As Joshua came to the edge of the waters of the Jordan, so the Church comes to the edge of revival rivers. These rivers are to be crossed. We are to dip our feet into the waters and then cross through the river, allowing the river to soak us, refresh us, and add to us.

When we come to the edge of these different streams, we should ask ourselves some pertinent questions: Is this revival river authentic? Does it have authentic biblical elements that we can spiritually discern? Does it have the ingredients of revival longevity—principles, truths, and leaders of integrity? If I cross this river, will the people of God receive from it and will we be able to handle it? What might I find in the river if I have eyes to see beyond the flowing waters, beyond the noise of the current, and beyond the refreshing that we will enjoy in the river?

All of the different revival rivers have truths to deposit in our churches that will cause us to move from visitation to habitation. God's desire is that the river flows into His house, the Church. Jesus moved from the countryside, from the streets, into a house (see Mark 2:1), and the house was full of people because Jesus was in the house. The revival rivers must move from conferences to churches, from large convention services to the weekly gatherings of God's people, from spiritual experiences to spiritual growth and maturity evidenced in both congregational life and family life.

Preserving the Stones without Polluting the River

How do we capture the Holy Spirit's truths from each of these revival rivers without damaging our churches, our families, and our ministries? What happened in Toronto was a humbling and spiritually enlarging experience for me and ultimately for our church, but I must add that we didn't become a "Toronto" church, nor did our church resemble the Toronto Revival. We did have repentance, weeping, and new tenderness toward the Holy Spirit. People were on the floor at times, but we still maintained our God-given river, the basic, discernible distinctives that we have built our church upon for many decades.

When we dip into authentic revival rivers, I believe these spiritual experiences, truths, or emphases should be assimilated into the river that God has already given each church. Trouble arises when we believe the unique model of another revival church or movement with a specific and unique revival river should become our new model.

Our particular local church is built upon what we discern to be biblical values or distinctives. For more than four decades, these distinctives have been proven to build healthy local churches with a continual flowing river of God. Seasonal outpourings of God's Spirit, like seasonal rains, have enlarged or added to our river, but we do have a river year-round.

Each revival river that I have mentioned, and several I haven't, has had some influence on our river because we journeyed to the edge of each river, dipped into the river, found some memorial stones, stones of truth that we could carry out of that river and deposit into our river. Even in so doing, we maintained our values and distinctives.

Values and beliefs are critical dimensions in church effectiveness because they serve as the basis for direction and action. According to management expert Philip Selznick, "The formation of an institution is marked by the making of value commitments and the institutional leader is primarily an expert in the promotion and protection of values."

You might be asking, "What are your values and distinctives?" Let me explain them simply and forthrightly.

Without Vision Values, Our Purpose Will Perish

Our vision is built upon our values. Vision provides the church with clear direction, bringing the future into focus and motivating all to become involved. Our vision is to be an effective instrument of God by raising up a local church in our region that will be restored to biblical pattern and power and will become an instrument for Kingdom purposes, a harvesting church that reaches and keeps the harvest. Our vision simply stated is:

Exalting the Lord by dynamic, Holy Spirit-inspired worship, praise, and prayer, giving our time, talents, and gifts as an offering to the Lord.

Equipping the saints to fulfill their destiny through godly vision, biblical teaching, and pastoral ministries, bringing believers to maturity in Christ and effective ministry, resulting in a restored triumphant church.

Extending the kingdom of God through the church to our city, our nation, and the world through aggressive evangelism, training leaders, planting churches, and sending missionaries and missions teams.

Vision is that which a congregation perceives

by the Holy Spirit as pertaining to God's purpose for them, thereby creating spiritual momentum, resulting in spiritual advancement and maintained through spiritual warfare. Our *vision values* reflect our belief system, our core convictions and our building stones to build healthy churches with year-round spiritual rivers flowing strongly. We hold in high regard these vision values. Without these values, the vision would be a dead letter, resulting in institutionalism. These values breathe life into the vision and sustain the quality of the vision. The following are the vision values we embrace.

Vision Values

Value God's Word. We believe that the Bible is God's inspired Word, the authoritative and trustworthy rule of faith and practice for all Christians.

Value God's Manifested Presence. Enjoying God's felt/realized presence is our passion as a church. We believe that God's presence is available to God's people as they follow the pattern of worship seen in the Psalms (see Ps. 22:3).

Value the Holy Spirit's Activity. Both in our personal and corporate lives as believers, we welcome the moving of the Holy Spirit. The baptism of the Holy Spirit and the gifts of the Holy Spirit are part of our basic belief system.

Value the Family. We express this commitment in our strong emphasis on family in preaching, teaching, available counseling, home-school programs, and a K-12 Christian school.

Value Dynamic, Spontaneous Praise and Worship. The believer's response to God's presence may be seen in energetic worship with clapping, lifting hands, and singing spontaneous, unrehearsed songs unto the Lord.

Value the Principle of Unity. We do not seek conformity, but we value unity of spirit and principle. A congregation may express itself in a variety of ways while maintaining unity in principles and convictions, flowing together to accomplish its vision.

Value the Holiness of God. Holiness is not like legalism that measures by outward appearance, but a true cleansing of the believer by the power of the Holy Spirit, which is evidenced in Christian character and conduct. The fruit is easily born forth.

Value Fervent Prayer and Intercession. We believe that intercession is the call of every believer. Therefore, the voice of prayer is heard as we pray out loud together in our opening service prayer times. We believe that the principle of prayer is the motor or powerhouse of our church life. Individual prayer and fasting and prayer for the whole church are continual and primary emphases.

Value Reaching the Lost. We believe that every believer is called to reach individuals who do not have a personal relationship with Jesus Christ. We are committed to remaining aggressive in reaching our entire city with the message of the gospel.

Value Excellence. We believe that God deserves the best that we have to offer; therefore, we seek to maintain a high quality of excellence in everything connected to the work of God.

Value Relationships. Our goal is to *love one another* and we endeavor to make this goal practical through small groups. Every believer is encouraged to develop deeper relationships with other believers that result in encouragement and accountability. This happens as we devote the times when we gather in small groups to both building and strengthening each other and reaching our community.

Value Integrity. There is no substitute for a lack of character. We hold this value in highest esteem and filter all other values through this one. Uprightness, trustworthiness, and transparency are essential foundation stones.

Value the Kingdom of God. We desire to positively influence the culture in which we live. We are to be salt and light to the world around us as we penetrate the political, social, and educational arenas with God's Spirit and Word.

Value Prophetic Ministries. We believe that prophecy and the ministry of the prophet are to be fully operational in the Church today. If the Church is going to be filled with vision and if it is going to operate under the full direction of Jesus, the prophetic voice must be heard. We do not accept that this and other ministries were to be confined to an "apostolic age," but that they are to be fully activated until the physical return of Christ.

Value the Local Church. We believe that the local church is the aspect of the Church that God is focusing on building in these days. Although we all recognize and understand that the larger Body of Christ encompasses all believers, all the plans and purposes of God are going to be demonstrated and fulfilled on the local scene. Every believer must find himself or herself in right relationship to God and to a specific local church to find a place of ministry and fruitfulness. It is essential that, rather than criticizing the Church, we do everything we can to make the Church of Jesus Christ glorious. The Church is God's instrument to extend His purposes on earth today.

Value Eldership Government. We believe that God has a plan and pattern for government in the local church. It is the same form of government God has used in every institution He has established. We refer to this as team ministry, or an eldership form of government, headed by a senior pastor or chief elder. This form of government involves equality and headship modeled in the Godhead, established in the natural family, set up by God in Israel, used in the synagogue, and ordained for the Church in the New Testament (see Acts 14:23; Titus 1:5; Heb. 13:17). The elders are to the local church what parents are to a family. They are the spiritual parents of the local assembly and are responsible before God to establish and equip the members of the church to be able to function in their God-ordained callings.

Value the Fivefold Ministry. We believe that the ministries listed in Ephesians 4:11 are to be fully functioning until the return of Christ. This includes apostles and prophets, not just pastors, teachers, and evangelists. All these ministries are needed if the Body of Christ is going to be properly equipped and the Church is going to be properly built up.

Value the Gifts of the Spirit. We believe that the gifts of the Spirit enumerated in 1 Corinthians 12:7-11 are for today and should be desired, sought after, and evidenced in every church. If there was ever a time that these gifts were needed, it is today. We do not believe that these gifts were intended only for the embryonic Church of the first hundred years. They are to be a part of the Church until the return of Christ for His perfected bride.

Value Unity and Diversity. We believe that every local church should be inclusive and actively seek to include all peoples of all races, ethnic origins, and socioeconomic standings. The Church of Jesus Christ is a multiethnic group that has within it the seeds for demolishing the scourge of racial prejudice. God's purpose is to make all people into one for His glory.

Revival, with all its intensity and excitement, should enhance our values, not diminish them or remove them. Values and beliefs are the foundation, the unchangeable, the guarantee for a healthy future. A church or movement must keep the core values to assure survival and success from generation to generation. These are so fundamental that, if a church is to meet the challenge of a changing world, it must be prepared to change everything about itself *except* these beliefs and values as it moves through different revival rivers.

The following eight steps state my own personal journey in coping with revival rivers as a pastor who has stepped into and drunk from each of the previous rivers we have spoken about.

Eight Stages to Revival Rivers

Renewal. The receiving of new Holy Spirit activity into a hungry soul and allowing the Holy Spirit to bring inner refreshing and remodeling of the soul as it seeks after God. Renewal is the receiving of new life and new fire into the soul of a person, a church, or a city.

Receiving. The attitude needed for leaders and people to receive from other streams of churches or movements. This is an attitude that rejects exclusiveness, knowing it is the strategy of the devil to keep movements apart, thus never allowing for cross-pollination. God's purpose for His Church is that we receive from others, even those who are very different. Having the attitude that resists everything new and thinks that "we have it all" is a sure way for a church or movement to become ingrown and ultimately suffer spiritually.

Refining. The process of clarifying past and present truths, principles, and biblical vision. When revival rivers are embraced and implemented into your own river, you must understand that revival truths or revival atmosphere might not correct a church's weaknesses. In fact, revival could expose the church's weakness and, if not dealt with wisely, bring harm to the church. Revival intensifies what is already present, so the refining process is of utmost importance.

Recovering. The ability to build upon previously laid foundations; keeping the old landmarks of truth is the guarantee of spiritual longevity.

Reforming. The process of matching new wine with new wineskins. New wine produced by revival usually necessitates time in the life of a church or ministry that embraces revival rivers. Change structure slowly for this is the bone of the church. Many churches are experiencing a restructuring crisis, the mobilization of lay ministry and small groups, and a decentralization of ministry. All of these must be done with biblical priorities.

Resisting. The spiritual warfare part of revival. Every revival has this, but it may be called by different names. Today's revival emphasis is on prayer, intercession, spiritual mapping, identificational repentance, and attacking strongholds in our cities. To implement this, a strong, healthy, local-church prayer base must be established with biblical knowledge about dealing with the unseen world.

Reaching and Reaping. This is the purpose of

revival, a breaking into the world of the unsaved, reaching our neighborhoods street by street until we reach whole cities for Christ. This reaching vision must be balanced with a securing of our personal, family, and church borders. Revival fires may burn hot in the church to reach the city, but the same fires may burn out the workers if we do not wisely secure our borders as we reach. Evangelism fire must be balanced with a pastoral heart for the individual, family, and every sheep in the flock.

Revival. This is not a word describing a special series of meetings or a spiritual experience by one or many. It is a word to describe the ongoing state of a healthy church, a church with a wide river, a river that takes in from other rivers, but maintains its own river distinctives. When biblical distinctives are maintained, a church may live with a powerful, fresh, flowing river of God.

Then he brought me back to the door of

the temple; and there was water, flowing from under the threshold of the temple toward the east, for the front of the temple faced east; the water was flowing from under the right side of the temple, south of the altar (Ezek. 47:1).

And he showed me a pure river of water of life, clear as crystal, proceeding from the throne of God and of the Lamb. In the middle of its street, and on either side of the river, was the tree of life, which bore twelve fruits, each tree yielding its fruit every month. The leaves of the tree were for the healing of the nations. And there shall be no more curse, but the throne of God and of the Lamb shall be in it, and His servants shall serve Him (Rev. 22:1-3).

The rivers of revival are moving. Let us not bypass, ignore, or react to them. Instead, let us approach the rivers with wisdom, vision, and values—a generation is at stake.

Reveal Your Glory
By Mark Strauss

Fill me with Your holy pow'r.
Touch me with Your Holy Spirit now.
Use me; Lord, I'm praying for the hour
When You reveal Your glory to me,
Lord.

Lord, I ask for a mighty rushing wind;
Lord, I seek for renewal deep within;
Lord, I knock 'til You open heaven's
door
And reveal Your glory to me, Lord.

Take me to Your hiding place.
Hold me; let me feel Your warm em-
brace.
I know I will see You face to face
When You reveal Your glory to me,
Lord.[6]

Personal Application

1. Revival rivers can bring both good and bad, but we must be careful not to throw the baby out with the bath water. Have you bypassed, ignored, or reacted to the river rather than reaching in and removing some stones of truth?

2. Reread the list of vision values. What are some of the value commitments you need to make?

3. Which of the eight stages to revival rivers (renewal, receiving, refining, recovering, reforming, resisting, reaching and reaping, and revival) do you need to adopt as you cross the waters?

NOTES

1. Winkie Pratney, *Revival Principles and Personalities* (Lafayette, LA: Hunting House Publishers, 1944), p. 11.

2. Hank Hanegraaf, *Counterfeit Revival* (Dallas: Word Publishing, 1997), p. 1.

3. Steve Hill, *The Pursuit of Revival* (Lake Mary, FL: Creation House, 1997), pp. 2, 3.

4. John Arnott, Malcolm McDow, and Alvin Reid, *Revival* (Nashville: Broadman Holman Publishers, 1996), pp. 148, 149.

5. C. Peter Wagner and Pablo Deiros, *The Rising Revival* (Ventura, CA: Renew Books), p. 13.

6. Mark Strauss, "Reveal Your Glory," City Bible Music, 1997. Used with permission.

Part 4

SELECTING RIVER STONES TO CARRY FORWARD

Take for yourselves twelve stones from here,
out of the midst of the Jordan. —Joshua 4:3

Joshua moved to the edge of the river and prepared the people for the long-awaited crossing. The crossing of the river for the people of Israel was the doorway to the fulfillment of their God-given vision to take the land and occupy it. They had wandered in the wilderness for 40 long years; a whole generation had lived and died in the wilderness and a whole generation was born in the wilderness. The generation born in the wilderness had more faith and vision for the new land than did its predecessors. They had only known wilderness, dryness, murmuring, and talk about the prophetic words from the past. Now it was their day, the day to cross over and begin to possess their destiny. The river crossing was the only experience left to endure before they would finally set foot on the land that would become their inheritance.

River Stones: Truths Discovered and Defined

The Israelites had no idea what was awaiting them in the land: walled cities, giants, testings, trials, battle after battle, casualties, death, and the loss of friends and family. The crossing of the river would introduce them to a new way of living and warring, a new culture. The river crossing would involve a strategy whereby the priests would find and remove 12 stones from the river and then carry them to the other side. This may not have seemed very significant at the moment of the crossing. It probably seemed like just more time wasted, more work to do—find stones, lift stones, carry stones and build stones into an altar. I'm sure that they were anxious to get on with the crossing of the river. What's so important about carrying stones at a time like this?

Every authentic revival river has hidden within it stones to be carried out of that river. Revival stones are truths discovered and defined as we journey through revival rivers. These stones must be kept relevant and alive in every generation as the truths discovered from the revival rivers. Joshua was to be careful not only to discover new stones, but to also keep the previous truths alive. Joshua 1:7, 8 records his instructions concerning the written law and Moses' previous words of instruction:

> Only be strong and very courageous, that
> you may observe to do according to all the
> law which Moses My servant commanded
> you; do not turn from it to the right hand or
> to the left, that you may prosper wherever
> you go. This Book of the Law shall not de-
> part from your mouth, but you shall medi-
> tate in it day and night, that you may ob-
> serve to do according to all that is written in
> it. For then you will make your way prosper-
> ous, and then you will have good success.

Joshua was to be careful to do all that was already written and to also discover 12 new stones
from the river he was to cross. We could liken the
law, or words of Moses, to our committed vision
values that should be word-based, timeless principles that we build on during all seasons. Leaders and churches today must know these biblically

based values and meditate upon them because our success and longevity is connected to these truths.

At the same time, we must not limit our future to what was discovered in the past. Our responsibility is to move forward and discover new stones of truth that we should carry out from this point forward.

Joshua 4:3 states our personal responsibility: "Take for yourselves twelve stones." Revival-truth stones are costly stones personally carried and protected by those who cross through the river. They are truths discovered in revival that are spiritually and personally embraced by the leader and the people. These revival-river truths become spiritual tools, convictions birthed and spiritually owned by the leaders and the people of revival.

"Take for yourselves twelve stones from here, out of the midst of the Jordan, from the place where the priests' feet stood firm" (Josh. 4:3). The priests' feet stood firm; the feet stood on dry ground, on a firm and stable place. Even though we pass through revival rivers, we must keep our feet on the dry ground of truth (Josh. 3:17). This dry ground is the ground of principles, doctrine, and objective truth, truths that become foundations, our belief systems. We stand on dry ground, resisting all opposition to past and present truth.

During revival seasons, the value of the subjective is usually heightened because the Holy Spirit is moving upon people's lives in a fresh and new way. As people encounter revival rivers, they are refreshed, renewed in mind and spirit, easily brought to repentance, and genuinely changed. The dry ground of objective truth balances the river of subjective experiences.

As we pass through these waters of various revival rivers, our responsibility is to find stones, truths that will outlast the experience, emotion, and intensity of the moment. Every revival must have a Bible base, a truth or truths that carry the revival. In the past, authentic revivals were marked by newly found truths: justification by faith, holiness, Holy Spirit baptism or infilling of the Holy Spirit, sanctification, gifts of the Spirit, missionary fervor, or new realms of prayer and fasting.

As we pass through the river, we must discover and define the river stones, not just the depth of the water, the power of the current, or the beauty of the flow. We must discover the foundational truths that validate the river as being authentic. These are the stones we must discover and then carry out for the next generation to remember and use as they build for the future. As spiritual leaders, we must "take up a stone on our shoulder" and bear these truths as personal burdens, if necessary. These truths may be controversial, causing others to attack the truth and the person carrying the truth.

Motivated by Love for the Next Generation

Our motivation must be the next generation. Revival stones are directional stones for the next generation. Joshua 4:6 says, "That this may be a sign among you when your children ask in time to come, saying, 'What do these stones mean to you?'" River truths are only fresh to the generation that first discovers and carries them on their shoulders. These same truths are not automatically accepted, respected, and kept alive by the next generation. River truths must be explained, imparted, and carefully placed into the next generation. Leonard Sweet, in his book *Eleven Genetic Gateways to Spiritual Awakening*, addresses this generational problem of spiritual decline in his denomination, the Methodists:

We suffered 48 percent loss in our market share in the past half century. If the chief purpose of a community of faith is to pass on its tradition to its children, we are facing a reproduction crisis of the highest order. The old prophecy—the church always stands one generation away from extinction—has almost been self-fulfilled.[1]

Leadership must carry river truths across every new era and every new river, laying them down in their new resting place, a new generation:

And the children of Israel did so, just as Joshua commanded, and took up twelve stones from the midst of the Jordan, as the Lord had spoken to Joshua, according to the number of the tribes of the children of Israel, and carried them over with them to the place where they lodged, and laid them down there (Josh. 4:8).

River stones discovered in the river must be symbolically kept in the river. The river of God's presence, anointing, and life must be the sustaining power of all river truths. If these truths were discovered in the presence and power of God, they must be kept by the presence and power of God. If river truths are separated from the river's power, they have the potential of becoming dead orthodoxy, dead letters without life-giving power. They may be documented and well-articulated, but, without the original power and life, they will not capture a new generation. The life of the teaching is in the life of the teacher.

There is a story of a spring of water that possessed extraordinary medicinal properties. Those who drank of its healing streams were miraculously cured of their diseases and infirmities. The news of this incredible find spread like wildfire, so multitudes came from far and wide to experience this phenomenal happening. Many erected homes beside the healing spring. Before long, hotels and businesses were also erected around the healing spring.

The town grew into a city, and the city became a great hub of activity.

Finally, there came a day when visitors would come to the city and ask, "Where in this great city is the pure spring of water that flows with healing power?"

With deep humiliation, the residents were forced to reply, "We are so sorry, but somehow in the midst of our progress and advancement, we lost the spring. Now, we cannot find it!" They lost the purpose of their existence.

The 12 stones taken from the river are spiritually quickened biblical truths—truths that may have lain dormant, but, by the power of the Holy Spirit, come alive during revival times. Listed next are the 12 stones that I have taken from recent revival rivers, as have countless other people. These are not the only stones to discover afresh from revival rivers, but they represent the renewed spirit of many people.

Twelve Stones from the River

1. The Stone of Humility and Simplicity

The Bible places a high value on humility and childlikeness. God saves (Ps. 18:27), sustains (Ps. 147:6), and gives grace to the humble (Prov. 3:34). Humbled before God, we are able to experience all the blessings He has for us. This stone is evident in every revival stream I have touched—stronger in some than others, but still present. Humility and simplicity, accessible to all who would see them as valuable, are God's gateway to receiving from any of His true servants: male or female, any race or color, small church ministry or large church ministry, clergyman or layman. All are conduits of God's Holy Spirit. When the disciples asked Jesus who was the greatest in the kingdom of heaven (Matt. 18:1-4), Jesus simply called to a little child and instructed the disciples to become like the child. Whoever humbles himself or herself like a child will be the greatest.

On several occasions at various revival hot spots, I have received from people who did not speak on the platform and were not visibly part of the leadership team. They were merely kind, gentle people filled with faith and desiring to be used of God as a channel of blessing. I must admit that my first thoughts were usually, "Who is this person and what can he or she do? This person is not even a full-time minister. How could this person understand my needs as a clergyman? What does this person have to give? I would rather have the keynote speaker pray for me. After all, does he or she realize who I am?" This way of thinking represents what the Bible calls pride, the opposite of humility, and is the attitude that hinders God from using others to bless us (Eph. 4:2; Phil. 2:5-8).

Leaders from all around the world have testified to the stone of humility and simplicity as a new truth or new experience for them. It breaks something down inside leaders. Their hearts are changed and this revival stone is used to provide a gateway to their own congregations (Rom. 12:3-16).

2. The Stone of Impartation

Impartation has taken on a new meaning for thousands of people in the last few years. Never have so many people been prayed for by so many people expecting to receive something. Impartation is biblical, with examples given throughout Scripture. Deuteronomy 34:9 says, "Now Joshua the son of Nun was full of the spirit of wisdom, for Moses had laid his hands on him." The impartation was real. It was tangible. Something happened to Joshua when Moses laid his hands on him.

In 2 Kings 2:9, we read, "And so it was, when they had crossed over, that Elijah said to Elisha, 'Ask! What may I do for you, before I am taken away from you?' Elisha said, 'Please let a double portion of your spirit be upon me.'" Again, we see the principle of impartation. Elisha expected to receive and Elijah had faith to impart from his life.

Impartation means to deposit, giving of something to another, or to place into (Gal. 1:16; 2:6). Romans 1:11 reads, "For I long to see you, that I may impart to you some spiritual gift, so that you may be established." The revival rivers flowing today have used this truth to minister to multiplied thousands. It is a revival stone we should pick up, put on our shoulders, and carry out of the river. There seems to be a new level of faith in people to receive from others, a new expectation.

3. The Stone of Intercessory Prayer

Everywhere you go, everywhere you look, you find books, CDs, seminars, conferences, magazines, churches with prayer pastors, prayer mountains, all-night prayer watches, and prayer movements. Prayer has moved to a new level. Prayer and intercession have been a part of all past revivals and certainly play a part of present revivals throughout the world.

The revival stone of intercessory prayer will revolutionize your life, ministry, and church. When I first came in contact with the different revival rivers, I was most overwhelmed with the spirit of intercessory prayer. The Holy Spirit would move thousands of people into a level of prayer and intercession that our church and I had not been previously experienced. As God dealt with me, and ultimately our whole congregation, we spent months teaching and practicing intercessory prayer.

We now open our services with 20 minutes of prayer and intercession in which the whole church participates and then we move into worship followed by hearing the Word. We have a prayer center, a prayer pastor and 400 trained and assigned intercessors. We picked up this stone, put it on our shoulders, and are carrying it out of the river.

Our mission statement concerning this newly discovered river stone of intercessory prayer is:

- Inspire every believer's heart toward prayer and intercession through the Word of God, stories, principles, and prayer models.

- Impart seeds of God's Word concerning prayer and intercession that will produce a great harvest of prayer.

- Impact each and every member of our congregation with a vision to change cities, nations, and history through prayer and intercession.

- Influence every believer toward prayer and intercession that stands in the gap and builds hedges for our families, churches, cities, and nations.

- Increase the faith of every believer to understand and utilize prayer as a powerful weapon to bring down spiritual strongholds and thus reap an awesome harvest of souls.

(Exod. 32:11-14; 1 Kings 18:41-46; Esther 5:1-3; Ezek. 22:30; Luke 2:37.)

4. The Stone of Reconciling the Generations

Each generation must receive its own distinct spiritual encounter with God. As generations come and go, they each bear certain dominant distinctions that are the result of cultural trends and spiritual powers. The Church is responsible for past, present, and emerging generations. We now face the rising of Generation Y, which was preceded by Generation X, the post baby boomers. Generation X has been called the "re-generation," which lacks identity and thus creates one by reviving or repeating the past. Whatever their identity, these young people—as do those of the following generation—desperately need an encounter with an authentic Christ, an authentic Church, and authentic spiritual mentors and leaders.

Revival fires have warmed the hearts of thou-

sands to reach these younger generations and reconcile past and present generations. There is a stone
in these present revival rivers, a stone of burden, intercessory prayer, and strategy from the Holy Spirit
to reach the next generation.

5. The Stone of Restoring Men to Take Responsibility

The revival that has taken place among the
men of our nation is both encouraging and chal-
lenging. This moving of the Holy Spirit will best be
sustained if we pick up this stone and carry it out of
the river—the stone of equipping and releasing men
into their God-called position.

No other group of individuals has more power
to shape or change the flow of history and spiritual life in our world today. If men do not receive
biblical training on how to take their place and fulfill biblical responsibility, we will miss what God
is seeking to do in our day. John Wesley's famous

proclamation was, "Give me one hundred men who love God and hate sin and we will shake the gates of Hell."[3]

Women have been marching along for 20 to 30 years with men standing by and watching the parade. God has certainly given men a wake-up call and it is of great importance that spiritual leaders pick up the stone of men's ministries, men's groups, men's training and men's roles in marriages and relationships and carry this stone out of the river. The men's revival must take place in our churches, not just in a stadium.

I have called the men in our church to pursue godly priorities. The following acronym of the word "Priority" serves as a guide and reminder to our men that we are pursuers of God (see Ps. 63:1-5).

Pursuing Our God: The command of Jesus was to seek first the kingdom of God. The psalmist says, pant after God, thirst for God

(Ps. 42), and seek God earnestly (Ps. 63). To pursue God is to practice the discipline of earnest prayer and to keep a single focus.

Rebuilding Altars: To build an altar is to express a special kind of dedication toward God. The altars we build are reflections of our spiritual state and attitude.

Investing Our Lives: Our joys, successes, and fulfillment in life are determined by the degree to which we discover God's purpose for our lives, invest ourselves in that purpose, and then use our talents, possessions, time, and energy to fulfill that purpose.

Overcoming Consistently: The power to overcome the habits of the flesh is found in understanding the right biblical principles and applying those principles by the power of the Holy Spirit. Victory is possible. It is promised in Scripture to those who discover and apply truth (Rom. 6:14).

Removing Obstacles: Long-standing obstacles must be removed in order for spiritual growth and progress to take place. Determine what they are, name them, and remove them. Common obstacles revealed in the Scripture are doubt, discouragement, rebellion, covetousness, an unruly tongue, and focusing on the pleasures of this life.

Invading Enemy Territory: Now is the time to go in and win back territory the enemy has taken in your life. Israel was given an inheritance in Canaan, but Joshua had to lead the people in and fight for it. Invading enemy territory takes vision, faith, and warfare.

Thinking Triumphantly: Train your mind to think godly thoughts based on the Word of God and inspired by the Spirit of God. Bad habits are the product of bad thoughts.

Yielding Successfully: Yield all ownership and rights to God, recognizing Him as Lord and yourself as His servant.

6. The Stone of Healing and Miracles

Most authentic revivals have borne witness to notable healings and miracles. The healing ministry has always been surrounded by significant controversy and, yet, it has been part of the Christian Church for centuries. Participants in revivals around the world maintain the belief that physical, mental, and emotional illnesses can be cured by the supernatural intervention of God through the prayer of faith. This stone must be grasped and held on to if we are to see healings and miracles move from the conferences and convention centers into our local churches.

The river of revival has come to reveal the stones in the rivers—stones to build with, not to walk over, forget, and neglect. The healing stone is desperately needed in every local church across this and every other nation. The power of the Lord to heal today is the same as it was in the day Christ walked upon the face of the earth (Isa. 53:5; Heb. 13:8).

The river of revival has refreshed our spirits and opened our eyes to this powerful stone lying at our feet. A stone of healing must be picked up by every leader and carried into the prayers of our congregations (Matt. 4:23-25; 8:7; 9:35; Luke 6:17-19). Many have crossed the rivers of revival before us, bearing the healing stone with awesome results: A. B. Simpson, Alexander Dowie, Charles Parham, Aimee Semple MacPherson, Dr. Charles Price, F. F. Bosworth, Andrew Murray, Oral Roberts, and many, many more.

Every local congregation needs a healing theology that is known and believed by the entire congregation. The following is one that I have used for years. It is simple and focuses directly on receiving your healing:

- Believe that healing is biblical, for today, and for you (Ps. 103:2; Isa. 53:1-3; Matt. 8:17; 1 Pet. 2:24).

- Believe that Christ's ministry of healing is now active through His people (Matt. 9:29; Mark 6:1-6; Jas. 1:6).

- Ask for the anointing of oil and prayer by the elders (Jas. 5:14; Matt. 6:13; Luke 13:11-13; Acts 28:8).

- Believe in faith that nothing is too hard for the Lord (Jer. 32:17; Matt. 8:2-4; 9:22, 29; 17:20; Mark 9:23; 10:27; 16:17).

Now, you must pray for the sick—continually, consistently, when it doesn't work, and when people deny it with thoughts like: "Oh well, I guess it's not for today." Peter Wagner says in his book *How to Have a Healing Ministry in Any Church*, "If people believe that God does not heal today, they will not be able to see divine healing, no matter what quantity of documentation or proof is provided."[4] Let us prayerfully and carefully carry this great stone from the revival rivers of yesterday and today.

7. The Stone of Holiness

Revivalists of the past have preached and written volumes on holiness. It is a new, fresh thought from the Holy Spirit for a new generation. Some of the holiness teachings of the past have resulted in a legalistic holiness that has been resisted by the emerging generations. Legalism that robs Christians of their true freedom in Christ is not the holiness of Scripture.

Legalism is an attitude. Although it involves code, motive, and power, it is basically an attitude. Legalism may be defined as a fleshly attitude characterized by an obsession with conforming to a code of artificial standards for the purpose of exalting self. Legalism, as an attitude, is founded in pride and results in manipulating rules for illegitimate control, requiring unanimity, not unity.

In most revival meetings I have attended, I have heard several testimonies about leaders releasing control. I believe control is linked to a legalistic spirit, a spirit that is deadened by religiosity and ministry driven by formality. When true Holy Spirit renewal invades a person's soul, this deadness is driven out and a new spirit of grace, mercy, and love takes residence with a new motivation for serving Christ and His people.

When grace fills a human soul, holiness becomes a vision, an automatic, new drive, and a desire to be free from anything that would hinder a first-love relationship with Jesus. Throughout the New Testament, the predominant thought is the grace of God in which Christ releases us, governs us, and gives a new hope and a new vision for our lives. As we see in Titus 2:11-14, the grace of God and the holiness of God are brought together in the believer's experience:

For the grace of God that brings salvation has appeared to all men, teaching us that, denying ungodliness and worldly lusts, we should live soberly, righteously, and godly in the present age, looking for the blessed hope and glorious appearing of our great God and Savior Jesus Christ, who gave Himself for us, that He might redeem us from every lawless deed and purify for Himself His own special people, zealous for good works.

Grace has appeared, bringing salvation and motivating the believer toward a new discipline—holiness. The Holy Spirit has once again enlightened our eyes to see this stone in the river so that we might pick it up and carry it over to the other side.

8. The Stone of Racial Reconciliation

John Dawson says in his book *Healing America's Wounds*, "America's cities are now the greatest gatherings of ethnic and cultural diversity the world has ever seen. We have inherited the wounds of the world, the clash of ancient rivalries, and we have our own unfinished business, particularly with Native Americans and Afro-Americans."5 The unfinished business that Dawson speaks about is racial reconciliation, a forgiving and reconciling of the injustices which races have incurred upon each other, whether from days past or present.

Second Corinthians 5:18-20 reads: "Now all things are of God, who has reconciled us to Himself through Jesus Christ, and has given us the ministry of reconciliation, that is, that God was in Christ reconciling the world to Himself, not imputing their trespasses to them, and has committed to us the word of reconciliation. Now then, we are ambassadors for Christ, as though God were pleading through us: we implore you on Christ's behalf, be reconciled to God."

This passage literally means that we have been called to be servants of reconciliation. Servants are those who yield their rights, submit to those over them and sacrificially give themselves to the cause. God has and is speaking forcefully and forthrightly concerning racial reconciliation; it is a stone of truth that you will find in present revival rivers.

Racial reconciliation is a God-word for this present time. As the world sits in racial hostility, the Church is being called to racial reconciliation. For some, this has been a hard stone to see in the river. Many think, "Not me, I've done nothing to these people. Should I need to ask forgiveness even though I wasn't present when they were enslaved, brutalized, or forced to give up their land? Why should I feel guilty?"

Of all people, Christians should be concerned about racial strife, conflict, and roots of bitterness. This issue is surely one of the most fundamental social problems of our time. In *Breaking Strongholds*, authors Raleigh Washington and Glen Kehrem quote Diane Sawyer's interview with Billy Graham on *Prime Time Live*: "If you could wave your hand and make one problem in this world go away, what would that be?" Without pausing for breath, Dr. Graham quickly replied, "Racial division and strife."[6]

The racial reconciliation stone must be picked up by every leader and every congregation. It is time to pick up our crosses, step out of our comfort zones, and build relationships across cultural barriers, beginning with at least one person, one family, one church.

When I finally understood and accepted this stone as a present truth, a Holy Spirit-inspired thought for the Church today, I moved toward making racial reconciliation a real livable truth for myself and our congregation. I needed to reconcile within my own heart first, "Yes, I am American and even though I wasn't here 200 years ago, my ancestors committed horrible sins against the Chinese, Japanese, Native American, and African-American people. This fact is part of my past, my heritage; therefore, it is my responsibility to ask for forgiveness and to work toward removing the hatred, the bitterness, and the long taproot of injustice."

I began with one African-American pastor, then two, then three, building relationships on a monthly basis through lunches, prayer meetings, city communion services, helping churches made up of other races with finances, staffing, legal help—anything I could do to strengthen the relationship between the races. It has been a learning experience. I, like many other white pastors, was totally ignorant of how to love the African-American, and I truly did not understand their frame of reference. I was frustrated and critical, thinking, "Surely, it can't be that bad. Why don't they just give it up? It happened 100 years ago!" The journey is still going on, but I am different now. I know how far we still have to go, but at least we have begun.

Racial reconciliation is one of the most important stones you will find in the river. Don't kick it or ignore it. Pick it up, own it, and carry it. Educate yourself. Begin by reading books and listening to tapes on the subject, or better yet, start where you are with one other person of a different race. I highly recommend reading *Breaking Strongholds* by Washington and Kehrem and *Healing America's Wounds* by John Dawson.

9. The Stone of Strategic-Level Spiritual Warfare

Spiritual warfare is not a new term to most Bible-believing Christians. True born-again believers understand that there is a real devil, who has real demonic forces at his command and wicked spirits in high places that wage war against people. Most Christians understand this kind of spiritual attack on a personal level, but many turn a deaf ear in unbelief when confronted with the concept that spiritual powers in high places control cities, regions, and nations.

Peter Wagner presents three levels of spiritual warfare in his book, *Warfare Prayer:*

First is ground-level spiritual warfare. This is the ministry of casting out demons as stated in Matthew 10:1: "And when He had called His twelve disciples to Him, He gave them power over unclean spirits, to cast them out, and to heal all kinds of sickness and all kinds of disease." Groups and individuals in deliverance ministries by and large are engaged in ground-level spiritual warfare.

The second level is occult-level spiritual warfare. It seems evident that we see demonic powers at work through shamans, New Age channelers, occult practitioners, witches and warlocks, Satanist priests, fortune-tellers and the like. Word that the number of registered witches in Germany exceeds the number of registered Christian clergy is startling. Hard data is elusive, but in all probability the most rapidly growing religious movement in America is New Age.

The third level of spiritual warfare is strategic-level spiritual warfare. Here we contend with an even more ominous concentration of demonic forces and powers—territorial spirits. This level of spiritual warfare has taken on new interest and new focus. City evangelism and strategic-level spiritual warfare becomes a top priority when taking our cities for Christ. The terminology that has surfaced over the last several years involves terms like spiritual mapping, breaking strongholds, city-reaching warfare, and strategic-level warfare, all of which have varying meanings to different people.[7]

Our journey into reaching our city has led us into prayer intercession, spiritual warfare, and spiritual strategies. When I first learned about spiritual mapping, I was, like many other believers, a little hesitant to put much stock in it. How can anyone use normal means to understand spiritual problems, spiritual strongholds, principalities, and powers? However, as we have researched and implemented strategic prayer and intercession, we have discovered that gaining a spiritual understanding of our city, region, and state has become very important.

Harold Caballeros, in his book *The Transforming Power of Revival*, tells the story of how spiritual mapping led him to understand the power over Guatemala. Guatemala had been offered and dedicated to a principality called Quetzalcoatl, the feathered snake. To begin spiritual warfare, one had to name the principality over the land that exercised its power through concepts, ideas, or ideologies (2 Cor. 10:3-5). Caballeros says that spiritual mapping is equivalent to intelligence gathering or espionage in war.[8]

Spiritual mapping is for the intercessors what an x-ray is for a doctor; it is a means for diagnosing the spiritual reality that affects our communities. This is precisely why we as leaders in our nation must pick up this spiritual stone: the stone of strategic-level warfare through strategic intercession. This is not an end in itself; it is a means to our end—evangelism, the winning of souls to Christ.

If you knew that spiritual mapping, along with prayer and intercession with balanced biblical warfare, would result in the tearing down of spiritual strongholds in your city and the releasing of souls from hell's grip, would you not use this weapon? I think you would because you desire to see souls come to Christ in every region. Obviously other ingredients are also needed to shake a city for Christ besides spiritual warfare on this level, but spiritual mapping is an effective weapon available to the twenty-first-century Church.

We Americans are deceived if we think spiritual mapping is needed more in the dark countries of our world—countries with witches, warlocks, curses, demons, pagan belief systems, idol worship—than in our own. Our nation is as dark, if not darker, than most. Spiritual powers are at work capturing the souls of people and where is the Church? The Church, for the most part, is content to stay within its four walls singing hymns to one another, running church programs, and speaking great messages against the darkness all around it.

We must strategically push back the invisible

powers, know what they are, where they are, and how to defeat them. This is a stone in the river that we cannot afford to mishandle. We must hold it tight and move on.

10. The Stone of Securing Total Freedom for Believers and Unbelievers

I have been in the ministry for over a quarter of a century serving as a youth pastor, associate pastor, Bible college professor, church planter, and now as the senior pastor of City Bible Church and president of Portland Bible College. My journey has allowed me to be on the ground level of new believers, new churches, new leaders, and new movements.

The one very vivid picture that stands out in my mind is the picture of someone bound with huge chains and crying out for help. As I walk around surveying this person, I try different keys to the locks. "No, not this key. Let's try this one. No. How about this formula?" This is a picture of frustrated spiritual leaders desiring to set people free, but not possessing the right keys.

Somewhere along the Church's journey, a significant part of Jesus' ministry has been dropped— His deliverance ministry, the ministry that set people free, broke the invisible demonic chains off people's souls, cast out demons, and broke off the spirits of infirmity. This part of Christ's ministry has been theologically assassinated and slowly, but surely removed from Bible colleges and seminaries. We teach young leaders how to preach, teach, administrate, counsel, and research, but when do we teach them the power of deliverance and how to set the captives free? Most see deliverance as an unpopular practice of ministry that can be replaced with psychology. Deliverance is not being practiced by many thousands of our American churches and the result is that thousands of both believers and unbelievers are living in spiritual bondage.

The Scripture says, "[We] will cast out demons" (Mark 16:17). Argentine evangelist Carlos Annacondia has modeled Jesus' ministry of deliverance and taking authority over evil spiritual powers. In his new book *Listen to Me, Satan!* on exercising authority over the devil in Jesus' name, Annacondia says, "Demons are evil beings who have no material bodies and they go around looking for a place to dwell. They speak, they reason, they see, and they hear."[9] Annacondia believes Jesus has given the believer authority to deal with these demonic forces that torment, oppress, or possess people. We have a great need to learn from this Argentine brother and many others south of the border.

Another approach to bringing total freedom to those suffering from chronic spiritual disorders is the Cleansing Stream Seminar from The Church On the Way, pastored by Jack Hayford.[10] The Cleansing Stream Seminar deals with finding and securing your freedom in body, soul, and spirit through prayers of deliverance, confession of sins, releasing bitterness, and tearing down strongholds of the soul. The Holy Spirit is using this approach to free many thousands of believers who have lived in some level of spiritual bondage.

Another trumpet-sounding message of securing your personal deliverance is *The Bondage Breaker* by Neil Anderson. In *The Bondage Breaker*, Anderson warns of our vulnerability to "very real and very personal demonic influences that are intent on robbing you of your freedom through temptation, accusations, deception, and control."[11]

Our culture is demonized, harassed, and tormented with multiple addictions to drugs, alcohol, pornography, and materialism. We must understand the absolute necessity for deliverance ministry. This river stone of truth must be picked up by local church leadership and placed into the local church congregation. Deliverance ministry should be part of the defined purpose and function of every local church. Deliverance counseling, deliverance prayer centers, and deliverance meetings are growing in our nation. Let us be wise and make room for this vital ministry under the covering of the local church.

Our local church eldership has spent months researching, reading available books, locating churches that have functioning deliverance ministries, and pounding out a basic deliverance ministry theology, philosophy, and function. Our basic line of thinking would be represented in this opening statement in one of our research studies given to the eldership of our church:

Demonology has been a controversial subject in the Body of Christ for quite some time. It seems that Christians tend to move to one of two extremes: either overemphasizing the existence and power of Satan and his forces, or denying or ignoring his existence and power. In some Christian gatherings, you may hear as much or more said about Satan and demons as about God and the power of the gospel. However, in other churches you would hardly ever hear a reference to the kingdom of darkness. We tend to either become demon chasers or powerless wonders. We are certainly in need of gaining a balanced perspective of the truth concerning this subject.

Our goal, however, must not only include becoming biblically informed (John 8:32), but also being spiritually empowered (Luke 10:19). We want the power of the truth and Spirit to permeate our experience, but we should not make the mistake of basing our doctrine on our experiences.

Our five senses and natural observations should be deemed inadequate to always accurately discern and define what is true in the spiritual realm, particularly in relation to the kingdom of darkness where the modus operandi is deception. Obviously, the Word of God is the only solid rock we have as the foundation for our understanding. May we be thoroughly equipped by it unto every good work (2 Tim. 3:16, 17).

11. The Stone of Reaping a Ripe Harvest, both Locally and Globally

The word "harvest" implies the season of gathering in a ripened crop, a time of reaping that which is mature. In Luke 10:2 Jesus pleads, "The harvest truly is great, but the laborers are few; therefore pray the Lord of the harvest to send out laborers into His harvest."

Positioning the Church for evangelism goes beyond implementing a program or hiring additional staff. Ultimately it takes a corporate change of heart. In my estimation, this is the purpose of the Holy Spirit's outpouring upon the Church: a change of heart toward the lost. The Church that does not reach the lost can be compared to a bread bakery that works hard to make bread, package bread, strategize the marketing of the bread while neglecting the starving, dying people looking through the glass at the bread.

A harvest passion will change our vision for ourselves, our children, our personal finances, our time, and our life goals. This passion will drive us from our religious comfort zones into a war zone, a place where we do battle for the souls of others. Our lives, our philosophies, and our values are deeply impacted and strategically changed by a harvest passion.

The Holy Spirit has quickened the following

harvest Scriptures so that we might meditate upon them and allow Him to use them to build a fresh new passion and faith within us for the ripened harvest:

> Then Jesus went about all the cities and villages, teaching in their synagogues, preaching the gospel of the kingdom, and healing every sickness and every disease among the people. But when He saw the multitudes, He was moved with compassion for them, because they were weary and scattered, like sheep having no shepherd. Then He said to His disciples, "The harvest truly is plentiful, but the laborers are few" (Matt. 9:35-37).

> "Let both grow together until the harvest, and at the time of harvest I will say to the reapers, 'First gather together the tares and bind them in bundles to burn

them, but gather the wheat into my barn'"
(Matt. 13:30).

"But when the grain ripens, immediately he puts in the sickle, because the harvest has come" (Mark 4:29).

"Do you not say, 'There are still four months and then comes the harvest'? Behold, I say to you, lift up your eyes and look at the fields, for they are already white for harvest! And he who reaps receives wages, and gathers fruit for eternal life, that both he who sows and he who reaps may rejoice together. For in this the saying is true: 'One sows and another reaps.' I sent you to reap that for which you have not labored; others have labored, and you have entered into their labors" (John 4:35-38).

And He said to them, "It is not for you to know times or seasons which the Father has put in His own authority. But you shall receive power when the Holy Spirit has come upon you; and you shall be witnesses to Me in Jerusalem, and in all Judea and Samaria, and to the end of the earth" (Acts 1:7, 8).

Then I saw another angel flying in the midst of heaven, having the everlasting gospel to preach to those who dwell on the earth—to every nation, tribe, tongue, and people (Rev. 14:6).

Churches in revival will dig into the river and find this precious "reaping a ripe harvest" stone, pick it up, hold it tightly, and carry it securely for it is foundational to the sustaining of revival in any city or nation.

William Carey, missionary to India, said, "Attempt great things for God. Expect great things from God."[12] The elements of contagious intensity and on-fire mission, impassioned with the task ahead, are what motivated heaven's Hall of Famers to give their all, even their very lives: George Whitefield said, "Give me souls or I will die."[13] "Now let me burn out for God!" cried Henry Martyn as he stood on Indian soil for the first time.[14] David Brainerd stated in his journal, "Consumed with passion for the pagan Indians, I cared not when or how I lived or what hardships I endured so that I could gain souls for Christ. While I was asleep I dreamt of such things, and when I awakened the first thing I thought of was winning souls to Christ."[15]

Jesus said in John 4:32, 34: "I have food to eat of which you do not know. . . . My food is to do the will of Him who sent Me, and to finish His work." This was His hidden source of spiritual nourishment, His hidden motor, His hidden well that He drew from continually.

The Church of the twenty-first century is in need of biblical passion:

- A passion that seizes harvest opportunities continually (John 9:35)
- A passion that views the harvest attentively (John 4:35)
- A passion that reaps the harvest aggressively (John 4:35)
- A passion that possesses the harvest immediately (John 4:35)
- A passion that labors in the harvest perceptively (John 4:36)
- A passion that loves the harvest deeply (John 4:36)

It has been estimated that we spend $600 on luxuries for every $1 we spend on missions. We have a nation that spends more on tobacco in one year than the United States and Canada combined has spent on missions since Columbus discovered America. Even if these figures are not exact, anything within reach of them is still staggering to comprehend.

A Harvest Philosophy

The Church must adopt a harvest philosophy:

- A philosophy that excites the believer to sharpen his or her sickle and prepare for the greatest harvest ever reaped in all of history

- A philosophy that believes the Church is a place of growth, power, and excitement; a place that God has ordained to become a force upon the earth—God is not pleased with evangelistic or missionary work that does not result in Church growth.

- A philosophy that propagates a positive approach to a negative society; a positive attitude of faith because the answer is found in Christ, and Christ is committed to the harvest

- A philosophy that believes in the ultimate victory and triumph of the Church as God's last instrument in His eternal plan and purpose; this plan involves the house being filled with souls from all walks of life.

- A philosophy that believes that, since God, as revealed in the Bible, has assigned the highest priority to bringing men into a living relationship with Jesus Christ, we may define our mission narrowly as an enterprise devoted to proclaiming the Good News of Jesus Christ and to persuading men to become His disciples and dependable members of His Church

- A philosophy that sees the world as God's harvest field—Therefore, all unreached people groups in the world must be reached with the gospel of the Kingdom. A people have been reached only when many of its members have become disciples of Christ and responsible members of His Body. Until the Church is well rooted in that society, it has not been reached.

- A philosophy that clearly understands and honestly evaluates all growth by asking these questions: Is it biological growth? Is it transfer growth? Is it conversion growth?

- A philosophy that handles the tension of the discipling and perfecting debate. Anti-growth attitudes that hinder the harvesting vision and spirit within the Church usually arise from confusion between "perfecting" and "discipling." The Church exists not for itself, but for the world. It always has a two-fold task: winning people to Christ and maturing people in Christ (Matt. 28:19, 20).

- A philosophy that believes that as Christ's servants, we shall stand before His throne eternally saved, but nonetheless accountable to answer for our stewardship of the gospel entrusted to us and the souls committed to our care and dependent upon our witness.

- A philosophy that believes that, at Christ's second coming and the resurrection of the dead, each human being shall be committed to either heaven or hell, dependent upon his or her reception or rejection of Jesus Christ

12. The Stone of Reaching Cities for Christ

An article in issue 23 of *Christian History* magazine about the First Great Awakening describes the impact of that revival upon Jonathan Edwards' town. In Edwards' own words:

The work of God: As the number of true saints multiplied, it soon made a glorious alteration in the town, so that in the spring and summer following, anno 1735, the town seemed to be full of the presence of God; it was never so full of love, nor of joy, and yet so full of distress, as it was then. There were remarkable tokens of God's presence in almost every house. It was a time of joy in families on account of salvation being brought unto them. More than three hundred souls were sovereignly brought home to Christ, in this town, in the space of half a year.

The First Great Awakening penetrated towns, villages, and larger cities, changing the way people lived, worked, and experienced church life. Today, in the midst of revival trickles, we are praying and hoping that the vision of our cities being penetrated by the power of the Holy Spirit will be fulfilled. City reaching has taken on a new force among thousands of pastors, leaders, and churches. Several influential leaders have been at the forefront of this truth. John Dawson and Ed Silvoso are two key strategists who have raised the water level on city reaching. John Dawson's book *Taking Our Cities for God* is one of the breakthrough books on this subject. Dawson speaks with boldness and insight about reaching cities:

> It is a sad, but undeniable fact that too many of us in the Church have been so charmed by the intellectualism of culture that we have supposed our strength may be in matching its materialistic lines of reasoning. Consequently, much of the Church has been shorn of its power in dealing with the invisible realm and thereby crippled for making grand and sweeping breakthroughs

in the arenas of deepest bondage and need—the world's cities. Like Samson, so many of us are bereft of power, shorn of its source, and blind to the reality of the invisible. Thus we 'grind at the mill,' plodding in circles like oxen, rather than moving ahead in spiritual power as sons and daughters of the Most High.[16]

The Church today is indeed floundering in the area of affecting whole cities for Christ, but change is coming. The Holy Spirit has raised up some men and women of God who are blowing their trumpets. Faith is being imparted to see entire cities and regions turn to Christ.

When I first began thinking about leading a whole city, I had not heard or read much about the concept. It was about 1980-82, and my wife and I were planting a church in Eugene, Oregon. I had very little training in the area of city strongholds, city personalities, city history, and spiritually mapping a city. None of these strategies were prominent at that time.

Now, more and more material is being written. Cities are being impacted today, whole communities changed by the power of the gospel. George Otis, Jr.'s book *Informed Intercession*, a guidebook on spiritual mapping and community transformation, lays out Kingdom principles that have not been widely exposed before now. Otis's research reveals the fact that transformed communities can happen:

> For some time now we have been hearing reports of large-scale conversions in places like China, Argentina, and Nepal. In many instances, widespread healings, dreams and deliverances have attended these conversions. Confronted with these demonstrations of divine power and concern, multi-

plied thousands of men and women have elected to embrace the truth of the gospel. In a growing number of towns and cities, God's house is suddenly the place to be.[17]

Ed Silvoso agrees:

The word is becoming clearer and clearer. The Holy Spirit is saying to the churches: Take the cities for God and bring them into My Kingdom. . . . We must continue our aggressive effort to evangelize nations and people groups and individuals and religious and rural populations, reaching unsaved souls wherever they may be found. But let's be clear: Nothing is more important in our day than reaching our cities.[18]

The stone in the river that we must not be intimidated to pick up is this one: Take your city on as your responsibility, your challenge, your calling. Thousands of pastors, leaders, and intercessors are becoming convinced that city reaching is indeed a spiritual reality. It will not be done easily or without casualties, work, prayer, and warfare, but it can be done and will be done.

I'll repeat my earlier warning: It is so important that river truths, or truths illuminated during renewal seasons, be carefully kept by the Spirit and not allowed to become mere orthodoxy or dead law. Scholarship must be balanced with spiritual life as truths are documented, articulated, and passed on to other people, movements, and coming generations.

The 12 stones of truth mentioned earlier are only representative stones. Others significant truths that you may choose to carry into your Canaan include prophetic gifts and leaders, extended fasting, lay ministry, apostolic ministry, prayer walking, networking, and cross-pollination.

The Spirit of God will guide you in your river

crossing when you seek His wisdom and strength. Look for river stones that will provide a strong foundation for this and future generations and allow God's presence and anointing to maintain their life-giving power.

Anointing

By Howard Rachinski

Anointing, fall on me.
Fresh anointing, fall on me
As I worship in Your presence;
As I bow down in holy reverence.
My desire is to see Your glory, Lord.
So anointing, fresh anointing fall on me.

I have tasted of your goodness and your mercy.
I have seen your faithfulness;
But my heart is longing for more.
Fill me with your holiness.

Purge me, Lord,
And sanctify this vessel;
Purified I want to be.
Holy fire burn away my weakness.
Let Your power flow through me.[19]

Personal Application

1. Are you willing to pick up stones of truth that may be controversial, causing others to attack you? What would some of those stones be in your church or denomination?

2. Have you picked up the stone of reconciling the generations? Or have you thrown stones of judgment at another generation? Would a kid lost in the grunge scene find an authentic Christ by getting to know you? If not, how do you need to change?

3. What have you done with the stone of racial reconciliation? Are you reaching out to someone of another race on a personal level? If not, will you commit to reaching out for Christ's sake in your community? And if you do not live in an integrated community, will you be the one to change it?

4. God is calling His people to a holy passion for

harvesting souls. What does your life—your checkbook, the way you spend your time, the way you raise your children, the way you set your goals—say about your passion for harvesting souls?

NOTES

1. Leonard Sweet, *Eleven Genetic Gateways to Spiritual Awakening* (Nashville: Abingdon Press, 1998), p. 17.

2. Barna Research Paper, taken from a pre-published manuscript.

3. Source unknown.

4. C. Peter Wagner, *How to Have a Healing Ministry in Any Church* (Ventura, CA: Regal Books, 1988), p. 143.

5. John Dawson, *Healing America's Wounds* (Ventura, CA: Regal Books, 1994), p. 23.

6. Raleigh Washington and Glen Kehrem, *Breaking Strongholds* (Chicago: Moody Press, 1993), p. 11.

7. C. Peter Wagner, *Warfare Prayer* (Ventura, CA: Regal Books, 1992), pp. 16, 17.

8. Harold Caballeros, *The Transforming Power of Revival* (Buenos Aires, Argentina: El Shaddai Ministries, 1998), p. 14.

9. Carlos Annacondia, *Listen to Me, Satan!* (Lake Mary, FL: Creation House, 1997), p. 45.

10. Timothy Davis, *Cleansing Streams* (Van Nuys, CA: Glory Communications International, 1995).

11. Neil Anderson, *The Bondage Breaker* (Eugene, OR: Harvest House, 1993), p. 13.

12. William Carey, source unknown.

13. George Whitefield, source unknown.

14. Henry Martyn, source unknown.

15. David Brainerd, source unknown.

16. John Dawson, *Taking Our Cities for God* (Lake Mary, FL: Creation House, 1989), p. 12.

17. George Otis, Jr., *Informed Intercession* (Ventura, CA: Regal Books, 1999), taken from a pre-published manuscript.

18. Ed Silvoso, *That None Should Perish* (Ventura, CA: Regal Books, 1994), p. 9.

19. Howard Rachinski, "Anointing," City Bible Music, 1998. Used with permission.

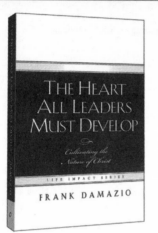

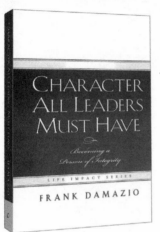

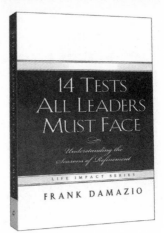

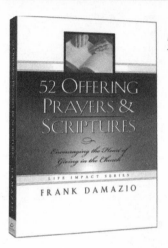

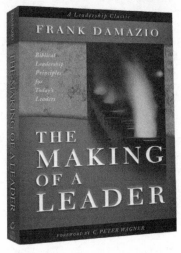

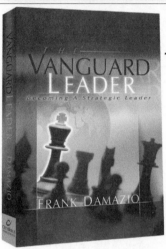

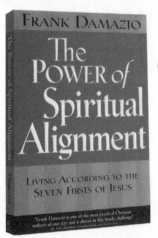